Cursive Handwriting Workbook for Teens

Practice Workbook with Fun Science Facts that Build Knowledge in a Young Adult

Legal & Disclaimer

The information contained in this book and its contents are not designed to replace or take the place of any form of medical or professional advice. The information provided by this book is not meant to replace the need for independent medical, financial, legal or other professional advice or services, as may be required.

The content and information contained in this book have been compiled from sources deemed reliable and are accurate to the best of the Author's knowledge and belief. The Author cannot, however, guarantee its accuracy and validity and cannot be held liable for any errors and/or omissions. When needed, further changes will be periodically made to this book. Where appropriate and/or necessary, you agree and are obligated to consult a professional before using any information in this book.

Upon using the contents and information contained in this book, you agree to hold the Author harmless from and against any damages, costs, and expenses, including any legal fees potentially resulting from the application of any of the information provided by this book. This disclaimer applies to any loss, damages or injury caused by the use and application, whether directly or indirectly, of any advice or information presented, whether for breach of contract, tort, negligence, personal injury, criminal intent, or under any other cause of action.

You agree to accept all risks of using the information presented in this book.

Cursive Handwriting Workbook for Teens: Practice Workbook with Fun Science Facts that Build Knowledge in a Young Adult

Introduction to Cursive Handwriting

The goal of this workbook is to help you develop or improve your handwriting skills. It is designed for beginners and intermediates since it mostly focuses on the cursive writing of entire words and sentences.

This book does, however, contain a short practice section for each letter. This overview includes recommendations on how each letter should be written. The rest of the workbook contains fun and interesting science facts from various fields like:

- *zoology*
- *paleontology*
- *geology*
- *geography*
- *astrology*
- *archeology*
- *and many more…*

Each exercise is composed of two parts. The first part contains specific words extracted from the sentence and written with a traceable cursive font. The second part contains a worksheet designed for the sentence to be rewritten in its entirety (multiple times if possible).

Learning the skill of cursive handwriting has numerous benefits. By pairing these benefits with the knowledge from the scientific facts, the value you get from completing each exercise increases radically.

Each science fact is short and easy to remember. The acquired knowledge can help you start interesting conversations with friends and family.

Cursive uppercase letters

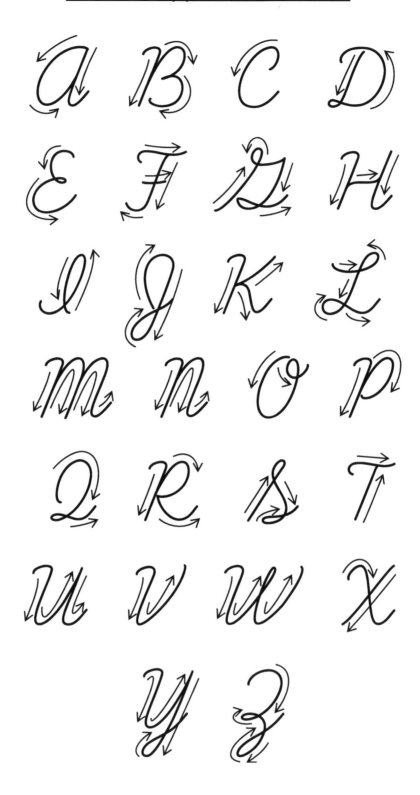

Cursive lowercase letters

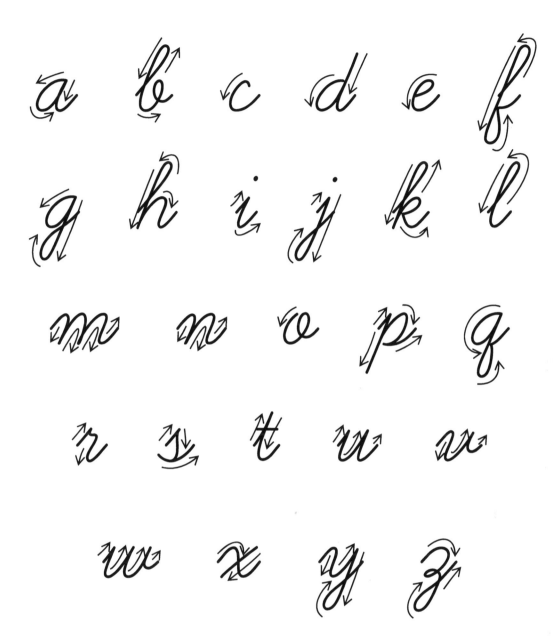

Cursive letter practice

e

F

f

g

g

H

h

l

i

j

j

K

k

L

l

m

m

n

n

O

$\mathcal{O}$

$\mathcal{P}$

$\mathcal{P}$

$\mathcal{Q}$

$\mathcal{Q}$

$\mathcal{R}$

$\mathcal{U}$

$\mathcal{S}$

$\mathcal{J}$

$\mathcal{T}$

t

U

u

V

v

W

w

X

x

Y

$\mathcal{Y}$

$\mathcal{Z}$

$\mathcal{Z}$

Science Fact #1:
Zoologists research the behavior, physiology,
classification and distribution of animals.

Zoologists

research

physiology

animals

Copy the entire previous quote below while using your best handwriting.

Science Fact #2:

Zoologists can also get involved in the conservation and the protection of endangered animals and their habitats.

involved

conservation

protection

habitats

Copy the entire previous quote below while using your best handwriting.

Science Fact #3:
Rabbits and parrots can see behind themselves
without having to move their heads.

Rabbits

parrots

behind

themselves

Copy the entire previous quote below while using your best handwriting.

Science Fact #4:
Despite its size, a hippopotamus can run faster than a man.

Despite

size

faster

man

Copy the entire previous quote below while using your best handwriting.

Science Fact #5:
Electric eels can cause electric shocks of around 500 volts.

Electric

eels

cause

shocks

Copy the entire previous quote below while using your best handwriting.

Science Fact #6:

The Cheetah is the fastest land animal on Earth. It can reach speeds of 113 km per hour (70 miles per hour).

Cheetah

fastest

animal

Earth

Copy the entire previous quote below while using your best handwriting.

Science Fact #7:
The Killer Whale, also known as the Orca, is
actually a type of dolphin.

Whale

known

Orca

dolphin

Copy the entire previous quote below while using your best handwriting.

Science Fact #8:
Cows and horses have the ability to sleep while standing up.

Cows

horses

sleep

standing

Copy the entire previous quote below while using your best handwriting.

Science Fact #9:
Female lions are better at hunting than male lions.

Female

lions

better

hunting

Copy the entire previous quote below while using your best handwriting.

Science Fact #10:

The Elephant is the largest land-based mammal on Earth.

Elephant

largest

mammal

Earth

Copy the entire previous quote below while using your best handwriting.

Science Fact #11:

Animals that primarily eat plants are known as herbivores.

primarily

plants

known

herbivores

Copy the entire previous quote below while using your best handwriting.

Science Fact #12:

Endangered species are those that may be completely wiped out if we don't offer them protection. They include blue whales, tigers and pandas.

protection

whales

tigers

pandas

Copy the entire previous quote below while using your best handwriting.

Science Fact #13:
The word dinosaur comes from the Greek language
and translates as 'terrible lizard.'

dinosaur

Greek

language

translates

Copy the entire previous quote below while using your best handwriting.

Science Fact #14:
Dinosaurs ruled our planet for over 160 million years.

ruled

planet

million

years

Copy the entire previous quote below while using your best handwriting.

Science Fact #15:

It is believed that dinosaurs lived on Earth until around 65 million years ago, when a mass extinction occurred.

believed

lived

around

occurred

Copy the entire previous quote below while using your best handwriting.

Science Fact #16:

A person who studies dinosaurs is known as a paleontologist.

person

who

studies

known

Copy the entire previous quote below while using your best handwriting.

Science Fact #17:

Birds descended from a type of dinosaur called theropods.

Birds

descended

called

theropods

Copy the entire previous quote below while using your best handwriting.

Science Fact #18:

Archaeologists study human societies that lived in the past. They discover and analyze the things that have been left behind by ancient civilizations.

Archaeologists

study

ancient

civilizations

Copy the entire previous quote below while using your best handwriting.

Science Fact #19:
Archaeology helps us understand how humans evolved and how different cultures developed.

understand

humans

evolved

cultures

Copy the entire previous quote below while using your best handwriting.

Science Fact #20:
A geologist is a scientist who studies the matter that constitutes the Earth.

geologist

scientist

studies

Earth

Copy the entire previous quote below while using your best handwriting.

Science Fact #21:

The hot liquid rock located under the surface of the Earth is called magma. Once it comes out onto the surface, it is called lava.

liquid

surface

called

lava

Copy the entire previous quote below while using your best handwriting.

Science Fact #22:

Natural gas doesn't have an odor. Humans add strong smells to it so they are able to detect leaks when they occur.

Natural

gas

strong

leaks

Copy the entire previous quote below while using your best handwriting.

Science Fact #23:
Copper is an excellent conductor of electricity and is commonly used for making wires.

Copper

excellent

conductor

electricity

Copy the entire previous quote below while using your best handwriting.

Science Fact #24:
Aluminum is a good conductor of heat and is,
therefore, commonly used to make cooking pots.

Aluminum

good

conductor

heat

Copy the entire previous quote below while using your best handwriting.

Science Fact #25:
Bronze is a metal alloy created from copper and
tin.

Bronze

created

copper

tin

Copy the entire previous quote below while using your best handwriting.

Science Fact #26:
Recycling old aluminum uses only 5% of the
energy needed to make new aluminum.

Recycling

old

energy

new

Copy the entire previous quote below while using your best handwriting.

Science Fact #27:
Recycling plastic can be more difficult than recycling other materials. Plastics are not typically recycled into the same type of plastic.

plastic

materials

typically

recycled

Copy the entire previous quote below while using your best handwriting.

Science Fact #28:
Glass is often separated into colors because it retains its color after recycling.

Glass

separated

because

retains

Copy the entire previous quote below while using your best handwriting.

Science Fact #29:
Oil and water do not mix under normal
conditions.

Oil

water

mix

conditions

Copy the entire previous quote below while using your best handwriting.

Science Fact #30:
Weather radars are used to detect tornadoes and give advanced warnings.

Weather

radars

detect

tornadoes

Copy the entire previous quote below while using your best handwriting.

Science Fact #31:

The world's largest desert is called the Sahara and it covers about one third of Africa.

largest

desert

called

Sahara

Copy the entire previous quote below while using your best handwriting.

Science Fact #32 :

The Nile River is the longest river on Earth. It has a length of 6650 kilometers (4132 miles).

Nile

River

longest

river

Copy the entire previous quote below while using your best handwriting.

Science Fact #33:

The highest mountain on Earth is Mount Everest. Its peak reaches 8848 meters (29,029 feet) above sea level.

highest

mountain

Earth

Everest

Copy the entire previous quote below while using your best handwriting.

Science Fact #34 :
The saltiest ocean located on Earth is the Atlantic
Ocean.

saltiest

ocean

located

Atlantic

Copy the entire previous quote below while using your best handwriting.

Science Fact #35:
The Earth is round and slightly flattened at the
north and south poles.

round

slightly

flattened

poles

Copy the entire previous quote below while using your best handwriting.

Science Fact #36:
The largest living structure in the world is the
Great Barrier Reef (located in the Coral Sea).

living

structure

Barrier

Reef

Copy the entire previous quote below while using your best handwriting.

Science Fact #37:
The Sun is over 300,000 times larger than the
Earth, with just 1% of its mass comprising of
oxygen.

Sun

over

times

larger

Copy the entire previous quote below while using your best handwriting.

Science Fact #38:
Scientists estimate that our solar system is
around 4.6 billion years old.

Scientists

estimate

around

billion

Copy the entire previous quote below while using your best handwriting.

Science Fact #39:
Oceans cover around 70% of the Earth's surface.

Oceans

cover

around

surface

Copy the entire previous quote below while using your best handwriting.

Science Fact #40:
The largest ocean on Earth is the Pacific Ocean,
which covers around 30% of the Earth's surface.

largest

ocean

Pacific

surface

Copy the entire previous quote below while using your best handwriting.

Science Fact #41:
The Pacific Ocean's name means 'peaceful sea'.

name

means

peaceful

sea

Copy the entire previous quote below while using your best handwriting.

Science Fact #42:
The Bermuda Triangle (also known as the Devil's Triangle or Hurricane Alley) is located in the Atlantic Ocean.

Bermuda

Triangle

located

Atlantic

Copy the entire previous quote below while using your best handwriting.

Science Fact #43:
Light travels from the Earth to the Moon in
1.255 seconds.

Light

travels

Moon

seconds

Copy the entire previous quote below while using your best handwriting.

Science Fact #44 :
Located in the Pacific Ocean, the Mariana Trench
is the deepest known point in the world's oceans.

Mariana

Trench

deepest

point

Copy the entire previous quote below while using your best handwriting.

Science Fact #45:

The temperature of the Sun's core is approximately 13,600,000 degrees Celsius. It takes around 8 minutes for the light from the Sun to reach the Earth.

temperature

core

minutes

light

Copy the entire previous quote below while using your best handwriting.

Made in the USA
Coppell, TX
13 August 2020

33305351R00057